An Artistic Collaboration

Poems by Joan Kantor

Artwork by Linda Anderson

ISBN-978-0-578-25240-7

WovenWord Press, Canton CT

Dedications

Joan:

I dedicate this work to my husband Chuck,
who has always been both an honest critic and my biggest
cheerleader. His unflagging support means everything to me.

Linda:

This book of poems inspired by my artwork is dedicated to
my daughter, Turiana, who has been a deeply rich influence in
my own life as I keep maturing. Thank you for being the
woman you are to me and the world.

Introduction

This collaboration between fabric artist Linda Anderson and word artist Joan Kantor came about quite serendipitously. They live on opposite coasts, had never met and had never seen each others' work. That all changed when Joan walked into an art gallery in Paducah Kentucky and saw Linda's art quilt, The March for Love.

Joan:

It moved me so deeply that I kept returning to visit it. I was in the middle of writing a poem about The Selma to Montgomery March, which was the subject of Linda's quilt. I jotted down Linda's information, hoping to see more of her work and to learn more about the quilt. The first image I saw when I went to her website was of Bringing You Home, an homage to her late husband. It brought back a powerful memory, and the words of a poem I'd written about my father's death forty years before. Thinking the artist would appreciate knowing the impact of her work, I reached out to tell her how much I admired The March for Love and how touched I was by Bringing You Home; I also sent a copy of that poem I'd written years before. In the meantime, I poured over the images of Linda's other quilts; the depth and emotional reach of them inspired me to write more poems. The emails began to fly back and forth with our mutual admiration for each others' work and the realization of the common threads that connected us as people, not just as artists. How lucky are we?

Linda:

One day in late May, I started the day with an email from Joan. She had seen my art quilt, The March for Love, in Paducah, KY., and was so moved by it, she looked me up online and viewed my Gallery page. She saw another work of mine, Bringing You Home, and was taken back to a poem she wrote 40 years before about her father's death. The poem perfectly matched my art piece, and she wanted to share how much my work resonated with her. I was so moved that a stranger would take the time to reach out and share how my work personally impacted her, I wrote her back with my gratitude and appreciation. That was the start of a most personal and intimate sharing of similar hearts and souls about humanity. She has continued to be drawn into my visual stories and responds with word art that leaves me speechless. What a rich way to add to the experience of art, combining words and visuals, in what I now know as ekphrastic poetry. A collaboration of like minds has been formed that has become a magical gift at this time in my life. How fortunate am I. What a woman of substance and heart she is.

Ekphrastic Poetry

Definition:

Ekphrasis is the Greek word for description. Over the years, the meaning of ekphrastic poetry has changed from being defined as descriptive writing. Though an ekphrastic poem can be a vivid description of a scene or, more commonly, a work of art, it can also be an emotional or intellectual response to artwork. Through the imaginative act of reflecting on a painting or sculpture, the poet may amplify and expand its meaning. There is much room for interpretation and storytelling in ekphrasis.

Ekphrasis in this Book:

You may notice that some of the poems have different titles than the works of art. At times, Joan chose to write a more descriptive poem, prompted by both the quilt and its back story. At other times, she let her imagination fly and came up with an alternative story that required its own unique title. Sometimes a different title just felt right to her.

Her Children
for Linda

She'll see a photo
or snap one of something
that others might not notice,
the happenings of life,
little intimate moments.
She has a vision
that sees beneath the surface,
a desire to create,
to share,
the passion and patience
to joyfully paint and stitch
for 50 hours a week,
the imagination
to tweak original images
just enough
to make them stand out.
The respect she has for her subjects
is in the carefully rendered details
of facial expressions,
fingers and hair,
in the constant switching of bobbins
and spools
to get the colors and contours
just right.
Compassion and connection exude
from each quilt,
the children she's birthed
from her heart.

The March for Love

"The March for Love"

dedicated to the memory of John Lewis

If they'd only had the courage
to look
with open minds
into the hopeful eyes
of this earnest young man
silently asking why,
his black face resplendent
with dignity
and the possibility
of offering forgiveness,
his head held high
above a sea
of peaceful protest,
before he was beaten,
before he chose
to get into "good trouble",
they might have found themselves
tossing their billy clubs aside
and reaching instead
      for the wide open hands
                of the future

Though the image in this quilt is not of John Lewis., for me, it represents the spirit of the man who famously participated in both the failed Selma to Montgomery March as well as the successful second one. Despite being brutally beaten, he used the words "March for Love" in reference to the march. He also coined the term "good trouble", which I interpret as the trouble resulting from action taken as a result of following one's moral compass.

Bringing You Home

Back to Life

I'm hollow
in this naked house
stripped bare
of him
of what was home

My father's gone
His hearth is cold

Beside his bed
an empty slipper waits

The mold of a familiar shape
fills again

Out steps the man

and joyful
I remember

This poem, written forty years ago, is the only one in this book that was written before I viewed Linda's work.

Remembering

Remembering...

She doesn't get out much these days.
Her aging knees keep her seated.
She chops the vegetables for dinner,
tells stories and tucks in the children.
She fills the emptiness of her days
with reminiscence and imagination,
as sitting beside the window
she creates a full life.
Pulling the curtain aside,
watching the world go by,
she homes in on the details
that trigger old joys:
children skipping on their way to school,
flowers blooming,
cars driving to places her imagination decides,
and especially couples holding hands.
The embroidery hoop on her lap disappears.
The walls become those of a dance hall,
as holding her young husband tightly in her arms,
she dips and swirls
to the pulsing memory
of passionate love
in her mind.

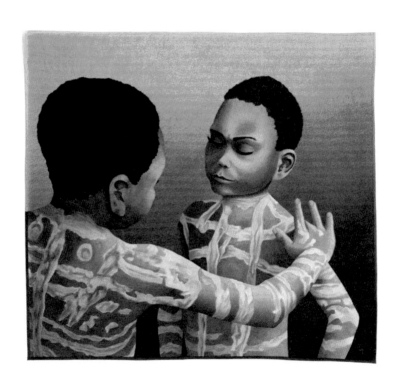

Becoming

Becoming

Two boys
preparing for a ceremony
are painting patterns of white
on each others' golden-brown bodies.
One of them,
full of anticipation,
stands perfectly still,
his brow furrowed,
eyes closed,
a sober expression on his face.
The other
Is tenderly completing the design
on his friend's shoulder,
and though we can't see his face,
we feel the warmth
and youthful wisdom,
the strength of the bond between them,
as leaning in
he tells his friend
there's nothing to fear,
that this ritual rite of passage
isn't all about strength,
it's also
    about having
            a heart.

Consuelo

Consuelo

She's bashfully smiling,
full of warmth and self worth
as she sits for yet another photo.
With skeins of yarn sitting beside her,
she holds a multicolored
unfinished weaving
in her equally colorful lap.
Though she's all dressed up
in traditional clothing,
something's amiss
as she sits
with her bare bronze legs
and swollen mud-caked feet
boldly stretched out
from beneath her skirt.
This woman is living
in two different worlds,
one for tourists,
the other for herself.

Maria's Tree

What We Don't Know

This naughty little girl
is standing barefoot on a bench,
while leaning in to secrets
leaking from an open door.
She knows they're not for her,
but frozen in place
she still listens to them all
and afterwards
will wish she didn't know
what she knows.
Once she was a joyful sprite
who danced around the house
in brightly embroidered dresses
that now starkly contrast
with the sadness in her face.
There's a disbelieving awareness in her eyes,
her once smiling full lips are turned down,
and as she grows
her parents will never know
why their carefree child
suddenly became withdrawn.

Spellbound

Spellbound

Surrounded by the hustle and bustle
of a busy marketplace,
this little boy sitting in a chair
with a book in his hands
is somewhere else.
Mesmerized,
he's been transported by pictures and words.
All distractions have vanished.
Though he's just learned to read,
he's already discovered the magic.

Reflecting

Reflecting

Untouched coffee now cold,
Slouching,
she sits by herself,
oddly glad to be so,
as she stares into time
passing her by.
Should she stay
or go?
Does it even matter
after 40 years together,
but alone?
She's learned to live with emptiness.
Is it too late to want more?
Is there someone else out there
with wrinkles, jowls and an open heart
longing
        to fill hers
                with love?

Velvet Flowers

The Thread

The fabric's been stretched.
the table frame set,
and these women gathered 'round it,
are stitching blue flowers
on black.
There's familiarity and a rhythm
to their work.
Equally comfortable
tossing gossip back and forth
or sitting in focused silence
while sewing,
knowing each other so well,
there's little need to talk.
They're separately together
doing their individual parts,
and a thread's connecting them all
to the whole.

In the Old Way

Who We Are

Women in Oaxaca Mexico
still sometimes dress little girls
in the colors and patterns of their villages,
telling stories
with the multicolored ribbons
they braid into their hair.
Though it's easy
to throw on a tee shirt and jeans,
there's no history,
no identity
in the weave.

Force of Nature

Force of Nature

She's a force to contend with,
using her heft
and an evil-eye stare
to keep the home crowd
in control.
The same children drawn
into the enveloping warmth
of her hugs,
the largesse of her love,
know the softness of her heart
can instantly turn to stone,
and the same hand reaching
to offer them sweets
could just as easily be reaching
to grab them
by the seat of their pants.

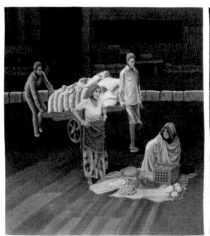

A Day in the Life

Invisible

In her faded pink clothing
and drooping headscarf,
the old woman sits
on a blanket
displaying her vegetables for sale.
With a clenched frown
and staring straight ahead,
she ignores the woman
telling her to move.

Later in the day,
chattering ladies
dressed to the hilt
stroll past where she sat.
It would be easy to forget
she was ever there,
if it weren't for the street sweeper
calling our attention
to the invisible crumbs
the woman left behind.

Pensive Pause

Inner Escape

Amidst the crowded chaos of India,
this woman is taking a break
from her street sweeping duties.
Having laid her broom aside,
she rests on the edge of a wall,
fidgeting with her fingers
while trying to tune out
the cacophony
of her surroundings,
hoping for one precious moment
away from it all,
to inhabit her soul.

Finding Comfort

Shared Strength

These boys,
though victims of trafficking
haven't lost hope.
They've grown to trust one another,
and carve out moments of camaraderie
in the sadness of childhood lost.
Huddled together,
they lean into comfort and courage
to get through one more day,
as uncowed,
they look straight ahead
toward the future.

Unbroken

Collateral Damage

somewhere in the war torn Middle East

During a break in the fighting
she looks through a shattered window,
an explosion or stray bullets
having disrupted one more day.
There's a sense of foreboding
in her deeply furrowed brow
as she wonders if or when
it will be safe to leave the building.
There's no milk, fresh vegetables, bread,
and the babies must be fed,
yet during this uncertain respite
does she dare make a run for the market?
What would happen to her family
if she never returned?
Is it even worth the risk
when there might be nothing left?
But what choice does she have,
when destiny's been rigged
to make women and children
the collateral damage
of men?

About the Artists

Linda Anderson

www.laartquilts.com

Linda earned a BFA and MFA in drawing from Otis Art Institute of Los Angeles County. She has one daughter, two step children and seven grandchildren. She taught art for six years, and then morphed into a few other careers over the next twenty five years as she raised a family. She, her husband and 10 year old daughter left the US in 1998 and went sailing, ending up in Trinidad and Tobago where they lived and worked for 10 years. Upon return to San Diego in 2009, she discovered the world of art quilts and immediately knew this was her future. It pulled her passions for painting and sewing together, plus an art quilt has the warmth of both hands touching, working and caressing it into creation. She is self-taught and has learned to paint all her fabrics to create the realism she is known for. Linda has received many first place, Best in Show, Outstanding Artistry, Judge's Choice and Viewer's Choice awards, both nationally and internationally. She was interviewed on San Diego's KUSITV in 2017, had a full page article in The Union Tribune Arts and Culture section in November 2016, and was selected as a "Star of San Diego' in January 2017. Linda's first book, What the Heart Feels, was published in 2021.

Joan Kantor

www.poems-photos.com

Award-winning poet Joan Kantor lives with her husband in the village of Collinsville, Connecticut. Joan was a college counselor and disabilities specialist for many years. She has been a featured reader for the public television series *Speaking of Poetry* as well as for several art museums and galleries, and she has also been a featured poet in *The Avocet Literary Journal*. Additionally, she leads workshops, has mentored for Poetry Out Loud, and has judged and mentored for the Hill-Stead Museum's Sunken Garden Poetry Festival Fresh Voices Poetry Program. To fulfill her inclusive vision of the arts, Joan collaborates with both visual artists and musicians and currently performs in *Stringing Words Together*, an interactive performance of poetry and violin music.

Joan's work has been widely published in literary journals and her first collection, *Shadow Sounds (*Antrim House 2010*)*, was a finalist in the *Foreword Reviews* Book of the Year Awards Contest (2010). She won First Prize for Poetry in The 2013 Hackney Literary Awards Poetry Contest and in 2015 her book*, Fading Into Focus*, took First Place for Poetry in The 23rd Annual *Writer's Digest* Self-Published Book Awards Contest. Her most recent collection, *Too Close For Comfort*, was published by Aldrich Press in 2016. She is currently working on two projects, *Dual Impressions* (original photos and poems), and *Filling in the Black* (a poetic recounting of her recent journey through the South, on a quest to re-educucate herself about African-American history).

Made in the USA
Middletown, DE
12 August 2022

70857707R00024